Life Processes

Anna Claybourne

Chicago, Illinois

www.capstonepub.com
Visit our website to find out more information about Heinemann-Raintree books.

To order:
☎ Phone 800-747-4992
🖥 Visit www.capstonepub.com
to browse our catalog and order online.

Edited by Andrew Farrow, Adrian Vigliano, and
  Diyan Leake
Designed by Victoria Allen
Picture research by Elizabeth Alexander
Illustrations by Oxford Design & Illustrators
Originated by Capstone Global Library Ltd

Library of Congress Cataloging-in-Publication Data
Cataloging-in-Publication data is on file at the Library of Congress.

ISBN: 978-1-4109-4423-8 (HC) 978-1-4109-4430-6 (PB)

Acknowledgments
The author and publisher are grateful to the following for permission to reproduce copyright material: Agefotostock: EA. Janes, 23 (bottom), Morales, 29; Alamy: Avalon/Bruce Coleman Inc, 20 (top), David B Fleetham, 19, Design Pics Inc, 5, 35, Jeffrey L. Rotman, 38; Getty Images: HuntStock, 11, Keystone-France, 39, Paul Souders, cover, Picsfive, 30, Ralph White, 27, Richard Clark, 32; Science Source: A. Barry Dowsett, 33, ADAM HART-DAVIS, 17 (top), ANDY HARMER, 37, BIOMEDICAL IMAGING UNIT, SOUTHAMPTON GENERAL HOSPITAL, 28, Francois Gohier, 23 (top), LEONARD RUE ENTERPRISES, 18, NEIL BROMHALL, 36, Power and Syred, 15, Scott Camazine, 25, WIM VAN EGMOND, 24; Shutterstock: Anatoliy Cherkas, 31, Birute Vijeikiene, 20 (bottom), Igor Janicek, 6, Johan Swanepoel, 8, Juice Verve, 41, Milos Ruzicka, 9, R-photos, 17 (bottom), Thierry Eidenweil, 13, zhukovvvlad, 16

Every effort has been made to contact copyright holders of material reproduced in this book. Any omissions will be rectified in subsequent printings if notice is given to the publisher.

Contents

Some words appear in the text in bold, like this. You can find out what they mean by looking in the glossary.

The Question of Life

What is life? It might seem obvious. But what life is and how it works is a big question for scientists.

Is it alive?

Think of a dog, a tree, and a mushroom. Think also of a human being, a spider, and a tiny germ that makes you sick. These are all living things.

But what about rivers, clouds, or lightning? They are not living things. But they are like living things in many ways. They can move, grow, and change.

And what about robots? They are built to act like living things. If they are intelligent, should they count as real life?

Different types of life

There are millions of different species on our planet. A species is a group of similar living things that can have young together. These species can be very different from each other.

But all living things have some basic things in common. They all use what we call the seven life processes. These are:

- movement
- respiration
- sensitivity
- nutrition
- excretion
- reproduction
- growth.

Turn the page to learn what each of these life processes do.

WHAT IT MEANS FOR US

Understanding life means understanding ourselves. It helps us cure disease and make medicines. Understanding life also helps us grow crops and help animals.

One of the most amazing sights in the animal world is a large flock of birds moving together.

Meet Mrs. Nerg

Whenever you need to remember the seven life processes, think of the pretend name MRS. NERG. This name stands for:

Movement
Respiration
Sensitivity
Nutrition
Excretion
Reproduction
Growth

WORD BANK
germ tiny living thing that causes disease
species group of similar living things that are able to have young with each other

The Seven Life Processes

If something performs all seven life processes, then it is a living thing.

What do they mean?

But what are the seven life processes? To start with, here is a quick guide:

Movement: All living things move.

Respiration: Respiration involves taking the substance oxygen from the air. A living thing uses this oxygen to create energy. Energy is the ability to do work.

Sensitivity: Living things pick up on what is around them. For example, plants and most animals notice light. This is called sensitivity.

Nutrition: Living things eat or take in food in some way. This is called nutrition.

Excretion: Excretion is when a living thing releases waste (leftover, unwanted substances).

Reproduction: Reproduction involves having young, or making new life.

Growth: All living things grow. This means they get bigger and develop.

Living things exist because of a variety of life processes.

The seven life processes in a pet cat

To see the life processes in action, think of how they work in a pet cat.

- *Movement*: The cat uses body parts such as muscles to run, lick itself, and so on.

- *Respiration*: A cat breathes in oxygen. This allows its body to perform respiration.

- *Sensitivity*: Cats can see, smell, and hear well. They also have senses of taste and touch.

- *Nutrition*: Cats hunt and eat meat.

- *Excretion*: Cats release urine (liquid waste).

- *Reproduction*: A male and a female cat can make baby cats, called kittens.

- *Growth*: A baby cat grows to full size.

	Cat	Cloud	Robot
Movement	x	x	x
Respiration	x		
Sensitivity	x		x
Nutrition	x		
Excretion	x		
Reproduction	x		
Growth	x	x	

Alive or not?

This table shows how only living things use all seven life processes. Some other things may have some of the processes, but they are not alive.

WORD BANK
oxygen substance found in the air
energy ability to do work

Movement

Different living things move in different ways. It depends on their surroundings and needs. Movement helps living things to find, reach, and take in their food.

Moving bodies

Some animals, such as cats or humans, move by using a system of bones, joints, and muscles. Bones give the body shape and hold it up. Joints are the connecting parts between bones. They allow movement. Muscles pull on the bones. This system is how we can make movements such as walking or picking up a pen.

A gemsbok can run at almost 40 miles (60 kilometers) per hour. This helps it escape attacks from other animals.

Movement methods

Creatures use different body parts to move. Birds and insects fly with wings. Fish use their fins and tails to swim. Bacteria are very simple living things. Some bacteria have
whip-like parts called flagella. Bacteria swish these flagella to push themselves along.

Plants and fungi

If left on a sunny windowsill, a plant will lean toward the sunlight. Daisy flowers open every morning. These are both examples of movement. Fungi are living things like mushrooms. They move by pushing their way up through the soil.

This climbing plant holds on to a fence post by wrapping itself around the post. This is a kind of movement.

Questions to think about

What would happen if nothing moved at all? Could a world of living things work that way?

Moving inside

Movement also happens inside a body. Organs are body parts that do particular jobs. The brain and heart are both organs. To do their jobs, organs often have to move. For example, your heart squeezes tight and relaxes with each heartbeat.

To stay alive, living things need to deliver things like food, water, and oxygen to their cells. (Cells are the tiny building blocks that make up living things.) They also need to carry waste back out. So, substances like water are always moving inside a living thing. For example, in
a human, food is squeezed along by the intestines (a tube-shaped body part). In a plant, water is sucked through the roots.

Intestines push food along. They tighten behind the food and push it forward.

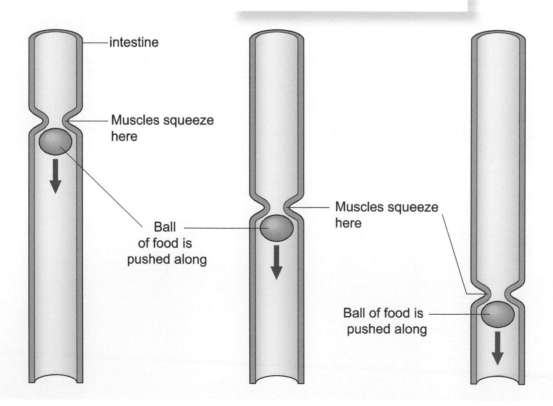

intestine

Muscles squeeze here

Ball of food is pushed along

Muscles squeeze here

Ball of food is pushed along

Problems

Germs and injuries can make movement difficult. For example, if you get food poisoning (caused by a germ), you may feel too sick to move around. Also, a broken leg will not work properly. That could mean the difference between life and death for a beetle escaping from
a hungry spider!

Today, we can replace some types of body parts if they are injured or missing. This man's artificial leg works so well he can use it for waterskiing.

Movement and health

Moving around is good for your health. It gives your body exercise. This keeps your bones, heart, and muscles strong.

Respiration

Respiration happens inside a living thing's cells. In the cells, oxygen and substances from food are combined. This process creates energy. This energy powers everything the living thing does.

How it works

This diagram shows how respiration happens in a shark. First, the shark takes in oxygen. It also takes in useful substances from food. Then, the shark's blood carries all of this to its cells. In the cells, energy is made and stored. Meanwhile, **waste** products leave the shark's body.

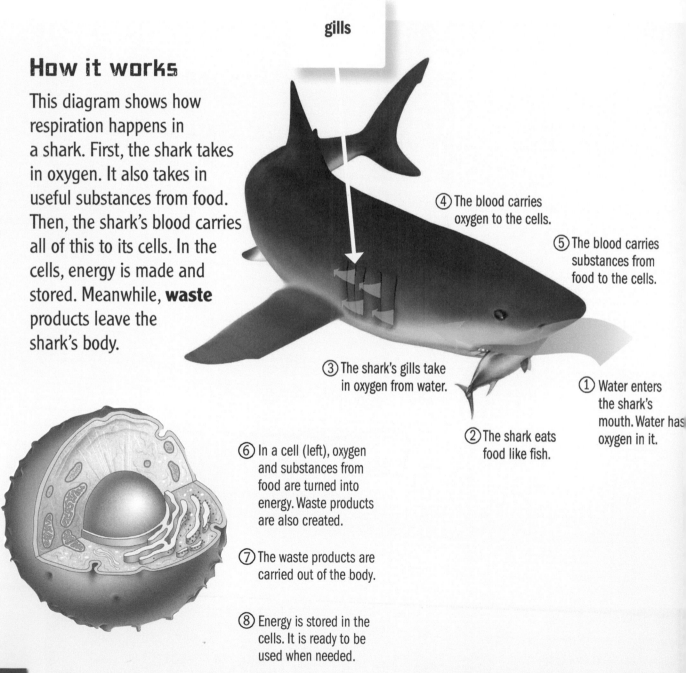

gills

④ The blood carries oxygen to the cells.

⑤ The blood carries substances from food to the cells.

③ The shark's gills take in oxygen from water.

① Water enters the shark's mouth. Water has oxygen in it.

② The shark eats food like fish.

⑥ In a cell (left), oxygen and substances from food are turned into energy. Waste products are also created.

⑦ The waste products are carried out of the body.

⑧ Energy is stored in the cells. It is ready to be used when needed.

How gills work

Most fish get their oxygen from the water around them. It comes through flap-like parts called gills. From there, the oxygen travels to the blood and cells. At the same time, waste products pass out through the gills.

This shows the gills of a whale shark.

Oxygen planet

Living things on Earth take in oxygen in many ways. Fish have gills. Humans have **organs** called **lungs** in their chests. These allow living things to survive in different surroundings.

WORD BANK
gills   organs that fish and some other water creatures use to get oxygen from water

Respiration in plants

Plants also need to create energy. They need this energy to perform life processes. So, respiration also happens in plants.

How it works

Plants let air into their leaves through little holes called **stomata**. Respiration then occurs inside the plant's **cells**. **Oxygen** from the air combines with a sugar called **glucose**. Glucose is stored in the plant. This process releases energy. It also creates the **waste** products water and **carbon dioxide.** Carbon dioxide is a substance in the air.

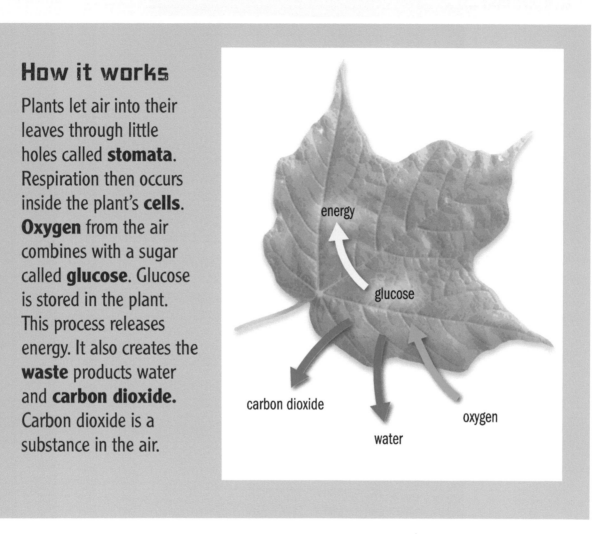

energy

glucose

carbon dioxide

water

oxygen

No oxygen?

Some living things turn food into energy without oxygen. This is called anaerobic respiration.

A few types of bacteria live this way. In plants and animals, it can happen when there is not enough oxygen. For example, when a runner sprints in a race, anaerobic respiration give his or her body a quick boost of energy. But this only works for a short time.

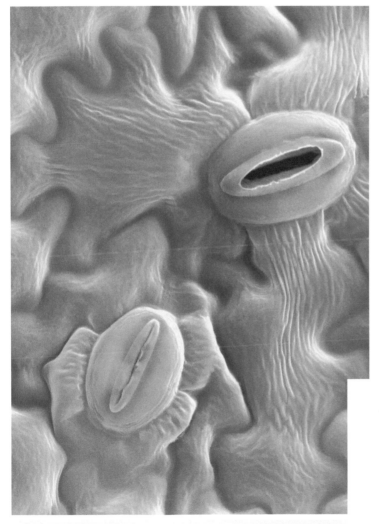

Bird breath

Birds need a huge amount of energy to power their flapping wings. They also need it to get off the ground. They can get this extra energy by taking in extra oxygen for respiration. Their **lungs** get a lot of oxygen from the air with each breath. They get more oxygen this way than most animals can.

These strange-looking shapes are stomata. They can open and close to let air in and out of a plant.

WORD BANK
stomata tiny holes in plant leaves that let air in and out
anaerobic respiration respiration without oxygen

15

Sensitivity

Sensitivity involves detecting (picking up on) surroundings. It also means responding to surroundings. Sensitivity connects us to everything around us. It allows us to move around and find food. It allow us to communicate (send messages). It also allows us to detect danger and make decisions.

Sense organs

Most humans have five senses. They are seeing, hearing, touching, tasting, and smelling. We have sense organs for each sense, such as our eyes and ears. Sense organs keep track of our surroundings. They also send signals to the brain.

Some living things have better senses than humans. For example, dogs and bears have a much better sense of smell. Some creatures have other senses, too. For example, a snake has heat pits on its face that can detect heat from animals it wants to eat.

This climber is using her sense of touch. It helps her get a good grip on the rock. Her sense of sight helps her find good holds.

Sensing light

For many creatures, detecting light is one of the most important senses.

See how your own eyes detect light. Go to a dimly lit room. Look in a mirror at your pupils. These are the small, round holes in the center of each eye. They should look quite large, as in the top picture below. This lets in as much light as possible, to help you see. Then, turn a bright light on. Watch as your pupils shrink, as in the bottom photo. This means they do not let in too much light. Your body senses how much light there is and responds.

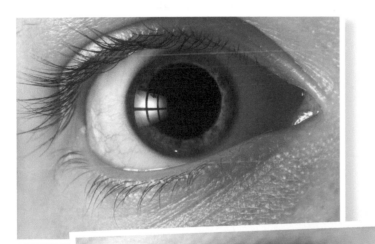

Questions to think about

Do things feel, look, or smell the same to everyone? It is hard to say. You cannot know exactly what other people's experiences are like.

WORD BANK
detect notice or pick up on
pupil small, round hole in the center of an eye that let light in

Sensing the world

Living things do not just take in information. They also respond to it. This could be something done on purpose. For example, if you see a coin on the floor, you might decide to pick it up. Your nervous system carries information to your brain. (The nervous system is the body system that senses things such as heat and carries messages around the body.) Then, your brain sends signals to your muscles.

Living things also have reflex responses. These are responses that happen without a person or animal thinking about them. For example, your eyes blink if dust flies at them. If a lizard's tail is grabbed, its nervous system causes its tail to fall off. This reflex may allow the lizard to escape.

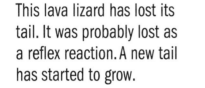

This lava lizard has lost its tail. It was probably lost as a reflex reaction. A new tail has started to grow.

Communication

The senses allow living things to communicate. Squid communicate by using flashing patterns of color on their skin. In this way, they use sight. Humans have developed spoken languages. They use hearing to communicate. Even bacteria can communicate with each other. They release special substances that other bacteria can sense.

These are oval squid. They flash fast-changing rainbow colors at each other to communicate.

WHAT IT MEANS FOR US

Medicines and other drugs can affect our senses. For example, alcohol (like beer and wine) dulls the sense of touch and pain. It also slows reaction times. Driving after drinking alcohol is dangerous. A drunk driver cannot respond to danger as quickly as usual.

WORD BANK
nervous system   body system that senses things and carries messages around the body
reflex   response that happens automatically

CASE STUDY

Blue Whale Versus Puffball Fungus

Over the next four pages, you can find out about two very different creatures—a blue whale and a puffball **fungus**. Compare them side-by-side. Both are living things. But they use their life processes in different ways. This lets them survive in very different surroundings.

The blue whale is the biggest animal that has ever lived.

Common confusions

Fungi and plants

Fungi, such as the common puffball, are not plants. They grow in the soil like plants. But they do not use sunshine to make food, as plants do (see page 26). Instead, they feed on rotting plant and animal material in the soil.

The puffball fungus is a type of mushroom.

Compare the creatures

	Blue whale	Common puffball
	The blue whale is a **mammal**. (Mammals are warm-blooded animals. They have backbones.) It lives in the sea.	The puffball is a mushroom (a type of fungus). It is found in woodlands and fields.
Movement	The blue whale has a skeleton (bones) and muscles. It powers itself through the water with its huge tail.	The **mycelium** is the underground part of the puffball. Its thin, root-like threads spread underground. Above ground is the large, ball-shaped "puff," called the **fruiting body**. This grows.
Respiration	A blue whale has **lungs**. It breathes in air and gets **oxygen** from It. This oxygen goes to its **cells**. In the cells, **respiration** turns food into **energy**.	The puffball fungus takes in oxygen. It goes to cells in its mycelium (see above). This is where respiration turns food into energy.
Sensitivity	Blue whales have a very good sense of hearing. They **communicate** with each other using very deep calling noises. They also have a good sense of touch. They cannot smell well, but can they can taste.	The fungus can **detect** food and water. It has no brain. This means it cannot see, hear, smell, or think.

WORD BANK

mycelium group of root-like threads that forms the underground part of a mushroom

fruiting body part of a mushroom or toadstool that appears above ground

Compare the creatures, continued

	Blue whale	Common puffball
Nutrition	Blue whales have filters in their mouths. These let water through. But they catch and keep the tiny sea creatures that are the whale's food (see the picture at top right).	The puffball feeds on rotting plant and animal material in damp soil. Its **mycelium** spreads out underground to reach food.
Excretion	The whale processes **waste**. It used its **lungs** and **organs** called **kidneys** to do this.	A puffball deals with waste through the process of **respiration**.
Reproduction	A male and a female whale **mate** (come together) to have young. The baby grows in the female's body.	The puffball grows millions of very small **spores** (seed-like parts). It "puffs" spores out into the air when it is touched (see picture at bottom right). The spores can grow into new **fungi** when they land.
Growth	A blue whale grows from a single **cell** inside its mother. When it reaches adult size, it can be up to 108 feet (33 meters) long.	The puffball's mycelium grows as it spreads out below the ground. The **fruiting body** grows to over 2 inches (6 centimeters) across. It is about 3½ inches (9 centimeters) high.

The filters inside a whale's mouth can separate food from water.

Life on Earth

As these two examples show, living things can vary greatly in size, appearance, and lifestyle. The ways their life processes work are also very different.

Scientists have already discovered and named around two million **species** of living things. But new ones are constantly being found. In fact, there may be many more millions of living things that we have not yet discovered.

When it is ready, a puffball "puffs" its tiny spores into the air.

WORD BANK
mate come together to have young
spore tiny seed-like part released by fungi

Nutrition

Nutrition means food. All living things need food. They use the helpful parts of food, called nutrients. This helps with energy and growth. It also helps with repair when parts of the body are hurt.

Eating and feeding

Living things take in food in various ways. Most animals eat with a mouth. Mouths can range from humans' jaws to birds' beaks. Some simple animals, such as amoebas, simply wrap themselves around their food and take it in. Plants can take in nutrients from the soil, through their roots. They also get food by using sunlight (see page 26).

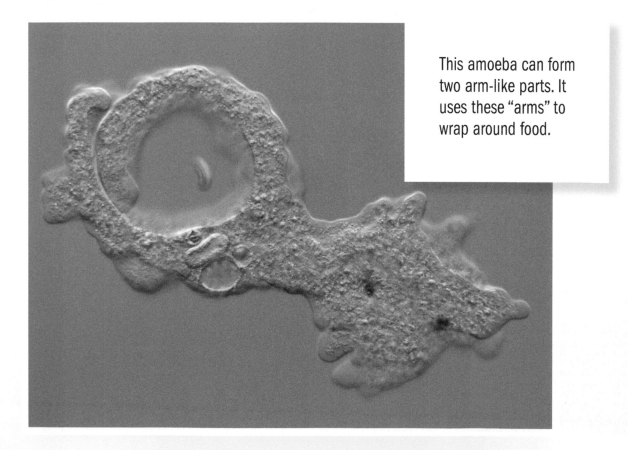

This amoeba can form two arm-like parts. It uses these "arms" to wrap around food.

Digestive systems

Many living things have digestive systems. These are body systems that break down food into useful substances. In humans, the food goes into the stomach. It then goes through the intestines, where it is broken down. Then the useful parts of the food are transferred into the blood. The blood carries them to where they are needed.

But digestion does not have to happen inside the body. Fungi release substances directly onto their food. This breaks the food apart. Fungi can then soak the food up into their cells.

In this X-ray, you can see a person's stomach (in yellow) and small intestine (in pink). The small intestine is tightly coiled up.

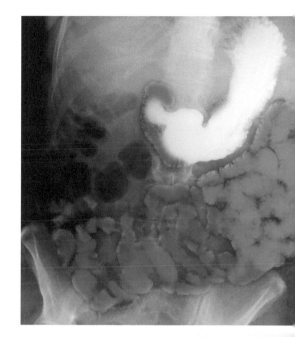

Waste

The parts of food that are not needed leave a living thing's body as **waste**. As an earthworm burrows through the ground, soil moves through its body. It gets the nutrients it needs from the soil. The rest comes out as waste. Some meat-eaters, such as owls, eat animals whole. They then throw up some of the waste parts (like fur and bones) in a lump.

WORD BANK
nutrient   useful part of food that living things use to live and grow
digestive system   body system that breaks food down into useful substances

Plant food

Most living things feed on other living things. But plants make their own food. They do this using sunlight, in a process called photosynthesis (see box below).

How does photosynthesis work?

Photosynthesis happens when a plant takes sunlight into its leaves. It uses the Sun's energy to combine water (sucked up through its roots) and **carbon dioxide** (from the air). This process takes place in leaf **cells**. It makes sugars. The plant uses these sugars as food. It also makes **waste oxygen** and water. These are sent out of the leaf.

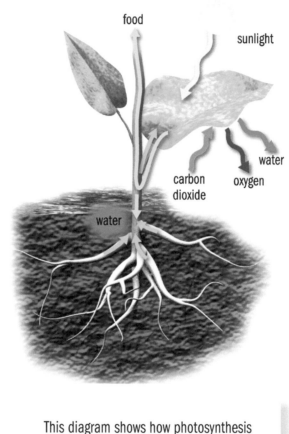

food

sunlight

water

carbon dioxide

oxygen

water

This diagram shows how photosynthesis happens inside a leaf.

Food chains

Food energy is taken from one creature to the next. This happens in a series of steps called a food chain. Food chains start with plants. Plants take in energy from the Sun in photosynthesis. This energy is passed on to animals that eat plants. It is then passed on to animals that eat those animals, and so on.

Life without light

Most food energy comes from sunlight, starting with plants. But there are some living things that do not need sunlight. Some **bacteria** deep underwater use special substances around them, such as sulfur, instead of sunlight. In this way, they make their own food.

Deep underwater, some bacteria do not need sunlight to make food. They can provide food for living things that live deep underwater with them, like these tubeworms.

WORD BANK
photosynthesis process plants use to make food, using light energy from the Sun
food chain series of steps of living things, each feeding on the one before

Excretion

Excretion happens when a living thing gets rid of waste.

What kind of waste?

During respiration (see page 12), carbon dioxide and water are produced. These waste products have to be carried out of the living thing. In humans, they come out through the lungs, as we breathe out. In plants, they escape through stomata (tiny holes) in the leaves.

Other types of excretion include sweat and urine. Sweat carries extra water and waste substances (especially salt). They leave out of tiny holes, or pores, in the skin. Urine removes extra water and waste substances from the blood.

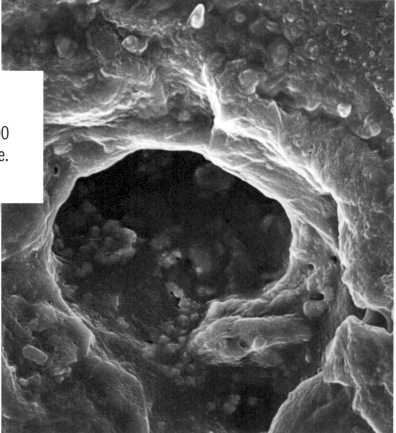

This is a human sweat pore. It is shown over 300 times larger than life size.

Useful excretions

Sweat serves another useful purposes. It makes our skin wet. This helps us to cool down in hot weather.

Urine has other uses, too. Animals such as dogs use it for marking their territory (area). Other animals can smell it. Scientists use human and animal urine to make some types of medicines.

The white crust on this marine iguana's nose is made from sea salt.

Sneezing lizard

The marine iguana lives on the Galapagos Islands, in the Pacific Ocean. Its body takes in salt from the seawater. It has a special **gland** on its nose. (A gland uses and releases substances from the body.) This gland gets rid of extra salt by sneezing it out. This gives the iguana a crusty white patch on its face.

WORD BANK
pore   tiny hole in the skin for releasing substances
gland   organ that processes and releases substances from the body

Staying balanced

After food and water enter the body, they are used in life processes. These processes create waste substances. Waste has to be removed. Otherwise it would build up in the body. The living thing would not work properly and would become ill or die. So, excretion keeps living things in a balanced, healthy state.

Using excretions

Humans can use the waste of other living things. One example is yeast. Yeast is a type of fungus that lives in groups. Yeast feeds on substances in sugars. It then releases carbon dioxide waste. We can capture the bubbles of carbon dioxide. This is what creates the bubbles in bread dough, which make bread rise.

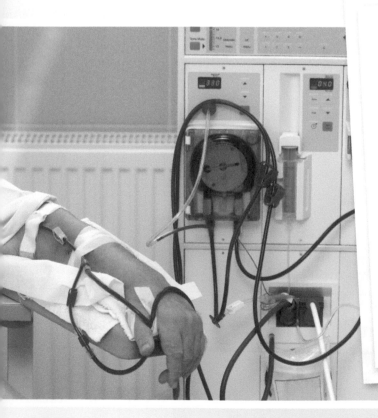

WHAT IT MEANS FOR US

The **kidneys** are very important **organs**. They remove waste from the blood. They also make **urine**. Urine takes waste from the body. If kidneys cannot remove waste, poisonous substances start to collect in the blood. These poisons can cause illness and death. People with failing kidneys need to have their blood cleaned by a special **dialysis** machine. This performs the job of the kidneys.

See for yourself

When it is very cold, you can see your own breath. If you breathe onto a cold surface, such as a window, it will become cloudy. The "cloud" is made from the waste water drops you are breathing out. This happens because your **lungs** release water into the air. Water is a waste product from **respiration**.

You can see your breath as a white-ish cloud on a cold day.

WORD BANK
urine liquid waste
dialysis filtering of the blood by a machine, to remove waste

Reproduction

Reproduction means making new life.

Sexual reproduction

In sexual reproduction, a male and female of the same species come together. They combine their cells to make a new cell. This cell can grow into a new living thing. For example, when they mate, a male elephant passes sperm cells (male reproductive cells) into a female's body. There, a sperm cell combines with an egg cell (a female reproductive cell). They form a new cell. This cell grows into a baby elephant inside its mother. It is then born.

This is a Highland cow with her calf. Cows use sexual reproduction.

Asexual reproduction

In asexual reproduction, there is only one parent. The parent makes exact copies of itself. It copies its own cells. This can happen in very simple creatures like bacteria. They reproduce by dividing in two. Some larger creatures also
use asexual reproduction.

These are *E. coli* bacteria. In the middle, you can see one bacterium stretching. It is separating into two new ones.

Strange snails

There are no male or female common snails. Instead, each individual is both male and female. When they mate, snails share their male and female reproductive cells. Both the snails then get pregnant (carry developing snails). They lay eggs. The eggs hatch out into baby snails.

WORD BANK
sexual reproduction   reproduction from the combination of a male and a female cell
asexual reproduction   reproduction from copying a single parent's cells

Plant reproduction

Most plants use sexual reproduction. For example, flowers have parts that release pollen cells (male reproductive cells). These travel on the wind or are carried by animals such as bees. They land on another flower of the same species. The pollen then meets the ovule (female reproductive cells). This creates a seed. The seed grows into a new plant.

Many plants can use asexual reproduction, too. For example, a single strawberry plant sends out stalks (long parts) called runners. The runners land in the soil and put down roots. They eventually become new, separate strawberry plants.

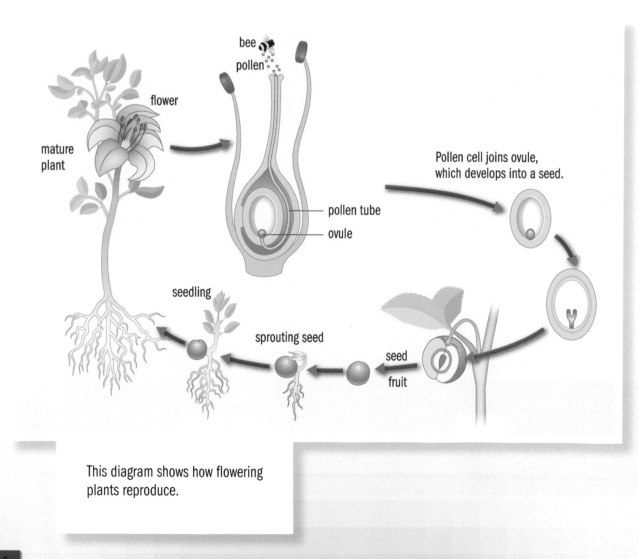

This diagram shows how flowering plants reproduce.

Passing on DNA

Deoxyribonucleic acid (DNA) is a substance found inside the cells of living things. The DNA acts as a code or set of instructions. It tells each species how to live and grow. When a living thing reproduces, its DNA is copied into the cells of the offspring (young). This is why offspring are always the same species as their parents. They have the same DNA.

Nature's clones

In sexual reproduction, the offspring is not identical to its parents. It is made from cells from both of them. So, it contains a combination of DNA from each parent.

But in asexual reproduction, the offspring is a **clone**, or exact copy, of its parent. It has exactly the same DNA. The parent's exact DNA is passed on in the cells used to make the offspring.

Identical twins share exactly the same DNA. So, they are just like clones.

WORD BANK

deoxyribonucleic acid (DNA) substance found in cells that stores coded instructions for how a living thing grows and lives

clone living thing that is an exact copy of another living thing and has the same DNA

Growth

All living things grow. Growing not only means getting bigger.
It also means growing things like hair and new parts.

Growing up

Some living things start life as single cells. Others start as small parts
of their parents' bodies. All types get bigger, until they reach the right
size for their species. Then, they are able to have young themselves.

This photo shows a human
unborn baby growing inside
its mother.

New cells

Living things grow by making more and more cells. This builds a bigger body. To make more cells, existing cells divide into two. Each new cell takes in food. It grows to the same size as the original cell.

But not all cells build up like this. Some cells, such as your blood cells, constantly die off. They have to be constantly replaced.

A new skin

Some creatures, such as insects and spiders, have a tough outer skin or shell. This is called an **exoskeleton**. It cannot stretch and grow. So, as the animal gets bigger, it must break out of its old skin and leave the skin behind. The animal then comes out with a new exoskeleton. The emperor dragonfly in this photo is leaving its old exoskeleton behind.

How big?

Most living things reach a maximum size for their species. They then stop growing larger. This happens as they reach adulthood.

The size of a species depends upon its body type and surroundings. For example, invertebrates (animals without backbones) normally do not grow very large. This is partly because they have no skeleton (set of bones) inside them to hold up a heavy body. But in the sea, where the water can support bodies, invertebrates can grow bigger. So, there are sea animals like giant squid and huge jellyfish.

This diver is with a giant spider crab. This is the biggest crab species in the world.

Limited growth

If living things don't get enough nutrients as they are growing, they can end up small. Diseases also sometimes make a living thing stop growing properly.

There are also hormones that affect how big or small a living thing grows. Hormones are substances in the body that control how a living things works. The tallest man ever recorded was Robert Wadlow. He grew to 8 feet, 11 inches (2.72 meters) tall. This was because of problems with his growth hormones.

The biggest living things

The biggest plants are the giant sequoia tree. They can be 295 feet (90 meters) tall. The biggest animal ever is the blue whale. It can grow to 108 feet (33 meters) long. It can weigh over 140 tons.

Robert Wadlow was born in the United States in 1918. He was the tallest human ever recorded.

A World of Life

So, living things need to perform the seven life processes to survive.

Processes in a cycle

The life processes are not separate. They work together. For example, for respiration to happen, a living thing must take in food. It needs nutrition. To get nutrition, it has to use sensitivity. Senses like sight help it find food. It also has to use movement to reach the food. Respiration and feeding create waste. This leads to the process of excretion. To power all these processes, a living thing needs energy. Energy is created by respiration. Energy also powers reproduction.

Life is everywhere

All the life processes are going on constantly. For example, at this moment bacteria are growing on your teeth. Dogs are barking. Someone is playing soccer. Butterfly eggs are ready to hatch.

See for yourself

When you do various daily activities, think about which life processes they involve.

For example:

brushing your teeth	running to catch a bus
eating an apple	going to the bathroom
reading a book	talking to a friend
playing a ball game	falling asleep

Questions to think about

Can you imagine a living thing that does not have all the life processes? Could it exist without movement, respiration, sensitivity, nutrition, excretion, reproduction, or growth? If it could, what might it be like?

At any moment in your everyday life, you will be surrounded by life processes.

Life Processes at a Glance

These two pages contain a quick reminder of all the life processes and what they mean. Don't forget to use "Mrs. Nerg" (see page 5) to help you remember what they are!

	Meaning	Examples
Movement	· Movement can mean walking from one place to another. It can mean plants moving petals as they grow. It can also be movement inside a living thing.	· Fish using their tails to swim. · A **fungus** spreading across the ground.
Respiration	· **Respiration** involves taking in **oxygen** and substances from food. These are combined in **cells**. This process helps change food into **energy**.	· Humans taking oxygen from the air into the **lungs**. · Plants taking in oxygen through leaves.
Sensitivity	· **Sensitivity** involves **detecting** surroundings by seeing them, feeling them, or in other ways. It also means responding to what is detected.	· A plant sensing a source of light. · A rattlesnake detecting body heat from an animal it wants to eat.

	Meaning	Examples
Nutrition	· **Nutrition** involves eating or taking in food. This provides a living thing with energy. It also gives it the **nutrients** it needs to grow.	· Tigers hunting and eating other animals, such as deer. · Plants turning sunlight into food energy using **photosynthesis**.
Excretion	· **Excretion** involves collecting and releasing **waste** from the body.	· Human **kidneys** getting rid of extra water and waste from the blood. · A plant releasing oxygen from its leaves.
Reproduction	· **Reproduction** involves making **offspring**. It makes new living things that are the same **species** as their parents.	· **Bacteria** splitting in two to make two new copies of themselves. · A male and female swan **mating**. The female then lays eggs that hatch into babies.
Growth	· Growth involves a living thing growing bigger as it gets older. It can also grow new body parts.	· A human growing from a baby into an adult. · A plant growing new leaves, flowers, and fruit.

Glossary

amoeba tiny, single-celled living thing

anaerobic respiration respiration without oxygen

asexual reproduction reproduction from copying a single parent's cells

bacterium (more than one: bacteria) type of very simple living thing

carbon dioxide substance found in the air and released as waste by body cells

cell building block of living things. It is the smallest unit of life.

clone living thing that is an exact copy of another living thing and has the same DNA

communicate send messages to each other

deoxyribonucleic acid (DNA) substance found in cells that stores coded instructions for how a living thing grows and lives

detect notice or pick up on

dialysis filtering of the blood by a machine, to remove waste

digestive system body system that breaks food down into useful substances

egg cell female reproductive cell

energy ability to do work

excretion collecting and releasing waste products from the body

exoskeleton tough outer shell or skin of some types of living things

flagella whip-shaped body parts

food chain series of steps of living things, each feeding on the one before

fruiting body part of a mushroom or toadstool that appears above ground

fungus (more than one:

fungi) type of living thing that includes mushrooms and molds

germ tiny living thing that causes disease

gills organs that fish and some other water creatures use to get oxygen from water

gland organ that processes and releases substances from the body

glucose type of simple sugar

hormone body substance that controls how a living thing works

intestine tube-shaped body part that carries food through the body

invertebrate animal without a backbone

joint connecting part between bones that allows movement

kidney organ that removes waste from the blood and makes urine

lungs organ in the

chest used in breathing

mammal warm-blooded animal with a backbone and fur or hair. Female mammals make milk to feed to their young.

mate come together to have young

mycelium group of root-like threads that forms the underground part of a mushroom

nervous system body system that senses things and carries messages around the body

nutrient useful part of food that living things use to live and grow

nutrition eating or taking in food. This provides a living thing with energy and the nutrients it needs to grow.

offspring babies or young

organ body part, such as the brain or heart, that does a particular job

ovule female plant reproductive cells

oxygen substance found in the air

photosynthesis process plants use to make food, using light energy from the Sun

pollen male plant reproductive cells

pore tiny hole in the skin for releasing substances

pupil small, round hole in the center of an eye that lets light in

reflex response that happens automatically

reproduce make offspring

reproduction making offspring—new living things that are the same species as their parents

reproductive relating to reproduction

respiration taking in oxygen and substances from food. These are combined in the cells. This process helps change food into energy.

sensitivity detecting the surroundings by seeing them, hearing them, feeling them, or in other ways. It also means responding to what is detected.

sexual reproduction reproduction from the combination of a male and a female cell

species group of similar living things that are able to have young with each other

sperm cell male reproductive cell

spore tiny seed-like part released by fungi

stomata tiny holes in plant leaves that let air in and out

urine liquid waste

waste leftover, unwanted substance

yeast single-celled fungus used to make bread

Find Out More

Books

Ballard, Carol. *Food Webs* (Living Processes). New York: Rosen, 2010.

Brasch, Nicolas. *Plant and Animal Survival* (The Science Behind). North Mankato, Minn.: Smart Apple Media, 2011.

Snedden, Robert. *The Scientists Behind Living Things* (Sci-Hi). Chicago: Raintree, 2011.

Somervill, Barbara. *Animal Cells and Life Processes.* Chicago: Heinemann Library, 2011.

Somervill, Barbara. *Plant Cells and Life Processes.* Chicago: Heinemann Library, 2011.

Spilsbury, Richard. *Life Cycles* (Living Processes). New York: Rosen, 2010.

Walker, Denise. *Cells and Life Processes* (Basic Biology). North Mankato, Minn.: Smart Apple Media, 2007.

Websites

http://faculty.washington.edu/chudler/amaze.html
Learn some amazing facts about animal sensitivity.

http://kids.nationalgeographic.com/kids/animals/creaturefeature/
Learn more details about all kinds of amazing animals.

www.biology4kids.com
Find detailed, wide-ranging information about many aspects of nature.

www.nationalgeographic.com
National Geographic's website provides more information about nature.

www.amnh.org
Explore the natural world on the American Museum of Natural History's website.

http://kids.discovery.com/tell-me
The Discovery Kids website has lots of information about the natural world.